European

This is the fourth insta
Europe

Exclusive discount for Patreon subscribers:
Sign up for only $1/month and receive an e-booklet in PDF
every month.

More info and download Vol I free at:

www.carolynemerick.com/books

Sign up at:

www.patreon.com/carolynemerick

Table of Contents

Illustration by Viktor Paul Mohn

"The Star Money" as a Quintessential Fairy Tale

"The Star Money" is a very short fairy tale found in the Brothers Grimm collection from Germany, but it surprisingly elicited a deep exploration for this series. Unlike other kinds of folktales, this story fits the pattern of a quintessential "fairy tale." In Volume III, we discussed some differences between folktale, fairy tale, legend, myth, and history. Fairy tales do fall into the category of folklore, but they are a specific sub-genre. Ironically, fairies are more often found in regular folktales than fairy tales. But, fairy tales will usually involve magic and the supernatural. Fairy tales usually depict a protagonist faced with some life crisis that they need to overcome. Very often, they embark on a journey to seek their fortune and/or destiny, although sometimes they face a challenge in some other way (such as being instructed to spin gold from straw). A typical fairy tale ends happily with the message that we can all overcome challenges and obstacles in our lives if we live as good people, are industrious, are kind to others, and so forth. Another common theme is that if we are behaving well, then supernatural aid will come to assist us.

Of course, there is wide variation, not all fairy tales fit the mold. And, some tales are difficult to differentiate whether fairy tale or generic folktale. A folktale will usually end abruptly. Folktale endings are often neither happy nor sad, they're just matter of fact. Although, a folktale is more likely to end sadly than a fairy tale is. A folktale might tell a story about a human's interactions with a fairy maiden, a mermaid, or a selkie, for instance. However, there is usually no set up to lay out a personal crisis before the meeting. Whereas a fairy tale protagonist may be an orphan, or a young person dealing with cruel or desperately poor parents and grappling for a better life and thus meets a supernatural helper on their quest, the general folklore protagonist often meets a supernatural figure completely at random. Where the fairy tale supernatural figure is often a guide who offers assistance, the general folktale supernatural figure may be helpful, malicious, or indifferent.

Illustration by Helen Jacobs

In this series thus far we have explored "The Three Heads of the Well" which fits the classic fairy tale pattern to a T. Next we explored "Per Gynt," which I would still classify as a fairy tale, but it deviates from the pattern in that the protagonist, Per Gynt, overcame his obstacles on his own without the aid of a supernatural helper. In fact, the trolls he was battling are more akin to general folkloric creatures. However, he does embark on a journey, he meets obstacles, and he overcomes them to meet a happy ending. This tale, more than not, fits the pattern of a fairy tale, but it does deviate from the quintessential pattern.

In Volume III, we discussed the tale of "Thomas the Rhymer." And, it was explained that the tale is difficult to categorize because there is historical basis for the person of Thomas, his story drifted into local legend, and then it carried on in the folk tradition. The tale was further altered as it moved from poetic form to ballad. And then Sir Walter Scott added additional verses to the ballad before it was reinterpreted in narrative form. "Thomas the Rhymer" somewhat fits the structure of a fairy tale as Thomas does go on a journey and he is given blessings by a supernatural figure.

However, he did not embark on his journey of his own volition, and he was facing no obstacle at the outset of the tale. Rather, Thomas was minding his own business, happy as can be, and was already the laird of his own castle (rather than a poor peasant who becomes a king or queen at the end). The supernatural figure appeared not to help Thomas along his journey, but rather kidnapped him against his will and hijacked him upon a journey. He was given blessings and gifts, but ultimately those gifts came with strings attached as he was required to return to the Fairy Realm when summoned.

So, this was a great example of how a tale can cross genres, and also how tales develop and alter over time. Some tales are truly rooted in history. In an oral society, one which records their history in the form of sagas and ballads which are then memorized and recited rather than writing them down, an historical event will eventually pass into legend and then into myth. Many folktales, such as described above where a protagonist has an interaction with a supernatural entity, are based on firsthand accounts that people claimed to experience.

This is not unlike modern ghost stories, urban legends, and accounts of alien abduction. A particularly interesting experience would make its way verbally throughout the village and beyond, exactly in the same way that modern urban legends still do. Over time, a tale can be influenced by other tales, be altered by the storyteller, and go through alterations resulting in variations. This means that we find many similarities among different folk and fairy tales, and why the same fairy tale can have sharp differences in different regions.

"The Star Money" is a quintessential fairy tale that fits squarely in the niche of the "fairy tale" genre. Like "The Three Heads of the Well," "The Star Money" features a young girl who is faced with a dilemma and embarks upon a journey to seek a change of fortune. The protagonist in this tale also meets beggars and, like the previous heroine, she chooses to share her own meager possessions with them. The girl in "The Star Money" is blessed for her generosity just like the girl in "The Three Heads," and likewise finds a happy ending. Although this tale is much shorter, it still follows the prescribed fairy tale pattern perfectly.

Europe's Cultural Roots in Ancient Indo-European Culture

When reading this tale, the main theme that I was struck with is that it is literally a lesson in Karma. Now, it might be instinctual to recoil at that word in an ancient European context as we consider it a foreign word native to Indian Hinduism. Of course, this is very true. However, an historical truth that many Westerners are oblivious to is that Europeans and Indian Hindus share a common linguistic and mytho-cultural heritage. I am not asserting the two groups are *closely* related or that they are remotely identical. However, both cultures stem from a Proto-Indo-European source, which is the modern term for what had always previously been referred to as "Aryan" historically.

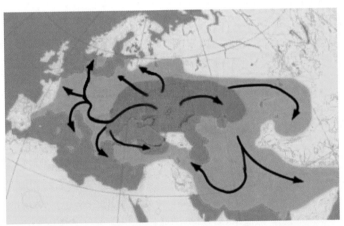

Indo-European migrations from ca. 4000 to 1000 BCE according to the Kurgan hypothesis, map by Joshua Jonathan

The Aryans were an ancient culture that is thought to have originated in the Eurasian Steppes (the area between Europe and Asia) before spreading outward in many directions. Proto-Indo-European is used to describe the language family as well as the cultures that descended from this group of people. The ancient word "Aryan" meant "noble ones," as they had been great conquerors and formed the ruling classes in regions as widespread as Europe and India, to Turkey and Iran.

A map showing the approximate present-day distribution of the Indo-European branches within their homelands of Europe and Asia, by Wikimedia user Hayden120

Iranian Persians were Aryans and Zoroastrianism is the ancient religion that developed in an Indo-Iranian (Aryan) cultural context. The Yazidi are an indigenous group found among the Kurds who still practice their ancient spirituality, and the Kalash people are a similar group who live in the mountains of Afghanistan. Both groups have Aryan origins, both groups feature a cultural inheritance that stands apart from the Muslim majority in their regions. Both groups have been heavily persecuted by their neighbors.

For Europeans, indigenous animistic polytheism (paganism) is our own ancient native religious inheritance which faced similar campaigns of violence during the Conversion Era of Europe (especially in the Wendish, Northern, and Baltic Crusades).

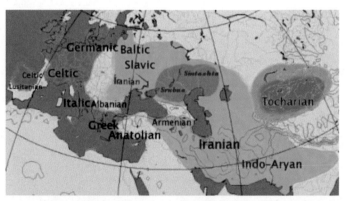

Indo-European language throughout Europe and the Middle East 500 BCE, by Wikimedia user DBachmann

So, therefore, while our own ancient religion did not have the ability to continue unabated in its full form, with temples, priests, and so forth, much of our ancient Indo-European beliefs were encoded and embedded within the folk tradition. The process worked differently for our Kalash and Yazidi cousins. Those groups survived as small pockets of tribal remnants who kept their culture intact, though sadly, they are at risk of true ethnic genocide today. But, it is in India where Aryan spirituality has been preserved in the most intact way within the Hindu tradition.

Proto-Indo-European is the mother language of both Sanskrit and most European languages. There are bits and pieces of European mythology that bear similarities to Hindu myth, and this is seen from Russia clear to Ireland.

When cultures split and diverge, we see certain commonalities in the most ancient elements of culture and then they begin to grow apart as separate and unique societies with individual differences. Of course, cultural diffusion can and does occur also, where cultures can adopt elements of a foreign culture through interaction by means of trade, conquest, enslavement, intermarriage, or geographical proximity.

Historians and anthropologists can look at a number of things to ascertain if cultural commonalities occur due to diffusion, shared origin, or pure coincidence. In the case of native European and Indian Hindu culture, linguistic studies can corroborate mythical ties to lend credence to the theory of very ancient shared cultural heritage.

As we saw in "The Three Heads," ancient mythical figures can manifest in folk and fairy tales. Gods and goddesses sometimes shift to a fairy or some other being that is supernatural without the overt conception of god-status.

A language tree of Proto-Indo-European Languages

This allowed ancient figures to carry on within the culture without disrupting the religious view of the ruling class (because we know that religious change occurred from the top down) which could land the peasantry in hot water with both church and secular authorities (which were often closely linked). Religion is often political, and that is as much true for previous periods of history as it is in our current epoch.

"Thomas the Rhymer" showed us that certain aspects of pre-Christian spiritual practice were still engaged in in post-conversion Europe. Thomas' journey and interaction with the Queen of Elphame demonstrates not only the continuation of a goddess figure who lingered on in the folk tradition, but that there was still an intuitive understanding of shamanic practice living on amongst the peasantry. And, reading "The Star Money," strikes one as an overt lesson in Karma.

West German stamp illustrating "The Star Money"

Did Europeans Have a Conception of Karma?

I am quite sure that most people would knee-jerk a response to this question with a firm "no, Karma is a Hindu concept." And that is very true. However, we have seen that Hinduism shares very ancient cultural origins with European mythical belief. We have seen that there are certain aspects of European folk belief that have very ancient mythic origins rooted in Indo-European origin. And, we know that the fairy tale tradition has roots that are far more ancient than scholars had ever previously been willing to entertain. Some tales are now believed to date as far back as 6,000 years.

Because it is the nature of oral tales to shift, evolve, transform, and for older tales to influence newer tales, I would argue that the fairy tale genre in general would have drawn on a bank of culturally understood concepts, figures, symbols, archetypes, and themes so that even if a tale was a new creation by a storyteller, that the teller would have comprised his tale with ingredients that had come before him.

The question of how much paganism lingered on in fairy tales is a bit complex. In my opinion, a great deal of pagan belief lingered on in encoded ways. It is my assessment that paganism did not actually die out at all, it remained active and vibrant among the common folk, only it was somewhat muted and disguised – it had to be, or it would have been extinguished by Church persecution.

It is quite clear that the European worldview became a hybrid one. Where Europeans viewed their identities as strictly Christian, they unconsciously held on

Illustration by Arthur Rackham

to pagan beliefs and even ritual practices found in folk traditions. And this hybrid nature is evidenced very strongly in folktales in which Christian elements were inserted into tales that had their origins in a pagan past.

So, returning to the idea of Karma, in European tradition we will never find that word. According to the "Online Etymology Dictionary," the word "Karma" originally evolved from the Proto-Indo-European root "*kwer*" which means "to make or form." It is related to the Old Persion word "*kunautiy*" meaning "he makes," and the Sanskrit word "*krnoti*" with the same meaning. The Sanskrit meaning of "karma" is "action, work, deed; and fate."

In "The Three Heads," the fairy tale which demonstrated a vestigial memory of the old Teutonic mythic figures called the Norns, we also explored the Germanic concept of Wyrd/Urd, which is similar to fate. In that discussion, we explored how the Teutonic view differed from the Greek view because the Germanic people did not view fate as fixed. To the Teutonic people (which includes the Germans, Anglo-Saxons, Dutch, Norse, etc), your fate was malleable and could be changed depending on your decisions and actions in life.

So, we can see a clear connection between Wyrd and the definition of Karma as "action, work, deed, and fate." Karma is most often discussed in the Buddhist view which asserts that actions in this life determine one's fate in the next life. However, we have just explored how Aryan cultural worldview was wont to travel, and as beliefs (and languages) travel, they invariably end up diverging and developing differently. The actual meaning of the origin of the Proto-Indo-European root for Karma matches very well with the concept of Wyrd.

The Norns by Lorenz Frølich

The Spread of Culture Across Distance

The Teutons were not the only European group with this kind of concept within their worldview. When it comes to the interrelated nature of various European cultures, you will find some very broad similarities and then some contrasts and differences, just as you will see with other neighboring cultural groups in other parts of the world.

Culture, like genetics and language, tends to exist on a continuum. So, in general, cultures who live closely to each other will share more similarities than cultures that are further apart (unless something unusual happened). Cultures that engage in a lot of exchange with another culture will be influenced through the interaction.

In general, I tend to view Mediterranean and Latin Europe as distinct from the more northern cultures from Britain clear to Russia. This is partly due to climate (which does influence culture), and also because the various cultures around all sides of the Mediterranean were heavily networked with one another.

For example, Greek and Roman culture influenced the non-European Mediterranean from Turkey to Israel over to Egypt in North Africa. Likewise, Middle Eastern and North African culture shared some features with Southern Europe, such as similarities in cuisine, in worldview, and so forth. For instance, the cult of Isis is distinctly Egyptian, but it was adopted by Greeks and Romans and temples to Isis could be found in Southern Europe during antiquity.

The Justice of Trajan by Eugène Delacroix

By contrast, Northern Europe, by which I include Teutons, Celts, Finns, Balts, Slavs, etc., although they were not completely isolated, they were less well connected with the on goings of the ancient world. They were linked up with trade networks, but they were not connected with non-European cultures to the same degree that Southern Europe was for the majority of their cultural development. So, in my view, there is a distinctly Northern European culture that runs on a continuum from the Celts and Teutons over to the Balts and Slavs. While languages and specifics may differ, you will find broad similarities as well. To be sure, you will also see similarities between Northern and Southern European cultures, but again, these things function on a continuum.

That said, many of the beliefs, traditions, legends, and holidays that we know from one Northern European culture have analogous examples in other Northern cultures which are simply not as well known in the English speaking world. For instance, we think of Halloween as a distinctly Gaelic (Celtic) holiday. And it is. It stems from old Celtic *Samhain*. However, the Norse, the Germans, the Balts, and the Slavs also celebrated at that time, they simply used different names unique to their respective language groups.

The same goes for most of the major holidays in the European tradition. And many of them stem from Aryan fire festivals related to the turning of the year – which is why many of these holidays are celebrated with bonfires in Europe even to this day. Interestingly, a friend from the Pashtun tribe of Afghanistan, which also has ancient Aryan roots, recently shared with me that his own culture celebrates fire festivals that include some of the same traditions seen in European festivals, such as fire jumping.

*Night on the Eve of Ivan Kupala, by Henryk Hector
Siemiradzki*

Why the Baltic Matters

It should not be surprising to find that the Baltic indigenous tradition has preserved a worldview that encompasses similarities to the Teutonic view. In fact, the Baltic culture acts as a bridge between the ancient cultures of indigenous European belief and Hinduism. And, because European indigenous belief was preserved in ways that can be less clear than the more completely preserved mythologies found in written cultures (such as Roman and Hindu), sometimes the elements are vestigial in nature, fragmented, or spotty. Therefore, it's useful to explore a wide range of European tradition to grasp a broader overview of a general European outlook, as well as zoom in on your particular culture of interest to study specifics.

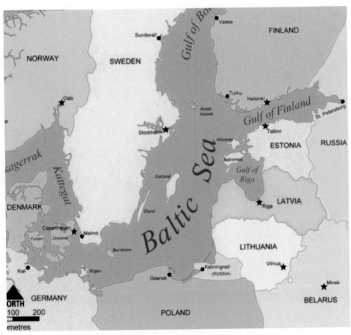

Map of the Baltic Sea by Norman Einstein

The Baltic is especially useful because of its geographic position. The region is nestled very closely to northern Germany, adjacent to Denmark, south of Finland on the Baltic Sea, north of Poland, just east of northeastern Russia. In other words, the culture exists at a crossroads of the Norse, the Finns, the Germans, and the Slavs.

Not only that, but it is a little known fact that the Balts were among the very last Europeans to convert to Christianity (other than very remote hold outs like the Saami people in Lapland and Mari in rural Russia). Many of us were taught in history class in school that the Norse were the last Europeans to convert. This is not true. The Norse converted later than the rest of mainstream Western Europe, but other groups held out much longer. Essentially, in orally based cultures, the earlier the tradition was wiped out, the less we are likely to know about it. The longer the belief system survives, the stronger the current of survival within the wider cultural context.

The Baltic was converted almost one thousand years after the Roman Empire adopted Christianity as its official state religion. Next came the Irish Celts, who are known for sending out missionaries into other parts of Europe. The Anglo-Saxons converted nominally in the 6th century, the Saxons by force under Charlemagne in the 9th century, and the Norse also by force in the late 10th century.

Many people do not know that crusades were launched by the Church against Europeans during the High Middle Ages. While the Middle-Eastern Crusades originated as a defensive maneuver to stave off constant attacks by Muslim armies, there were also crusades launched by Europeans against other Europeans for the sole purpose of spreading religion. The Baltic was attacked in large scale campaigns known as the Northern and Baltic Crusades, and the Slavs were attacked in the Wendish Crusades.

Of the Balts, Lithuania and Prussia were the last to be conquered and forcibly converted in the early 13th century. At that time, there had been a great pagan temple called the Temple of Romuva located in Prussia. The crusade was led by the Teutonic Knights from Germany, and that is why the name Prussia is remembered today as an ethnic-German country. Old Prussia was culturally Baltic and the people would have spoken the Baltic Old Prussian language.

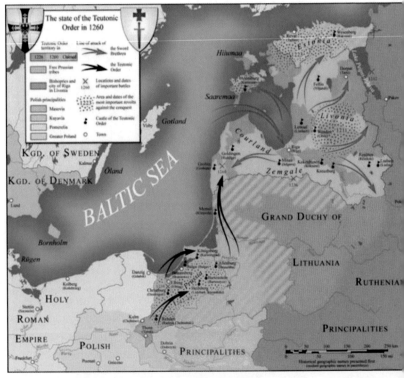

Map of the Teutonic state in 1260 by Wikimedia user S. Bollman

In recent times, as people of all ethnic groups of Europe (as well as many ethnic groups outside of Europe) work to reconnect to their ancient cultural roots, paganism has been revived in the Baltic, just as it has among Celtic, Teutonic, and Slavic people. The Lithuanian version of indigenous spiritual revival took their name from the Old Prussian pagan temple, the last great temple of pagan Europe, Romuva.

Romuva sanctuary in Prussia, a depiction based on a16th century account

The Baltic is a very important, but also very overlooked, region when it comes to gaining a broad understanding of European spiritual belief. Not only did their indigenous spirituality live on for hundreds of years longer than elsewhere, but the Baltic culture is said to be one of Europe's most ancient – i.e. it has closer ties to Proto-Indo-European roots.

In fact, the Baltic language is said to be the European language most closely related to Sanskrit. It is for this reason that the founder of the Romuva movement, Jonas Trinkūnas, has encouraged Baltic pagans to look to Hinduism. In fact, as leader of the Baltic pagan movement, he recognized the link to Hinduism and he worked closely with Hindu leaders over the years.

Jonas Trinkūnas, leader of Lithuanian pagan revival. Photo by Wikimedia user Thegoatman.

Why is this relevant? Number one, we just circled back to Europe's ancient Indo-Europe tie to another Aryan culture (India). And two, while I would never assert that any two European cultures are identical, in fact they do have marked differences, I would absolutely say that there is a broadly European culture that often transcends the various cultures despite their differences.

The only caveat is that I would put the Northern European cultures of Celts, Teutons, Slavs, Finns, and Balts much closer together and group Southern Mediterranean Europe closer together. (The Finns are not linguistically Indo-European! They are one of the few outliers, though they will share cultural similarities by way of cultural diffusion due to geographic proximity to the Norse, Balts, and Slavs).

So, since much of the European pagan tradition was lost (outside of what lingered on in folklore and folk customs), it behooves us to look at a close neighbor to help flesh out an understanding of a European concept of fate and "karma."

A pattern of the world tree, Austras Koks ("Tree of Twilight"), also commonly used as a symbol of Romuva.

The Baltic View of Fate

As we've been exploring the linguistic and mythical ties between ancient Europe and ancient Hinduism, and have noted that the Balts are said to be the European culture with the strongest ancient ties to its Indo-European roots both linguistically and mythologically, it is very interesting to note that among the core tenets of indigenous Baltic worldview is a belief in harmony.

In his short booklet, "Baltic Religion Today," Jonas Trinkūnas explains that the Baltic word for harmony is "Darna." He says that:

"The world is harmonious, but that harmony isn't regular, it sometimes weakens and disappears, therefore it is important to hold on to it, to create and expand it. A person's duty is to reach for harmony, to protect it."

A reconstructed pagan observatory in Šventoji, Lithuania.
Photo by Kontis Šatūnas

Later in the book he explains further:

"The depths of Baltic culture hide the idea of Darna (harmony). This is the root of many important concepts, expressed in the roots of such Lithuanian words as 'daryti, darbas, derlius, derėjimas, dermė, dora' (to do, work, harvest, to go together, concord, morality)."

Now we can compare the Lithuanian word "darna" with Hindi "dharma." Looking again at the Online Etymology Dictionary, we see dharma defined thus:

In secular sense, "caste custom, right behavior;"
in Buddhism and Hinduism, "moral law,"
from Sanskrit, "law, right, justice,"
related to dharayati "holds,"
and cognate with Latin firmus "strong; stable,"
figuratively "constant, trusty;"
all from PIE root *dher- "to hold firmly, support."

So we can see a clear tie between Baltic "darna" and Hindu "dharma" in terms of moral world view and righteous personal behavior. Jonas Trinkūnas goes on to explain other points of Baltic belief that bear striking resemblance to Hindu belief. For example, he says that:

The world is eternal. It is continuously created by the eternal godly powers. According to Lithuanian mythology, the world is created and re-created by at least two gods—light and darkness, creation and destruction (Dievas and Velnias). Their relationship created harmony and vitality.

To anyone with a cursory understanding of Hindu and Buddhist worldview, the above paragraph will be strikingly familiar. This describes the concept of Yin and

Yang, as well as the concept of cosmic cycles that are discussed in the Hindu Vedas. There are other similarities in cosmological worldview as well, but as our purpose here is to discover if Europeans had their own concept of Karma, without any such word, Trinkūnas it very well:

The most important aspect of morality (the golden rule) teaches that one must do unto all other living things what they would want to be done unto them, i.e. never do anything that you wouldn't want done to you. The Balts call this type of morality humanism. This is the avoidance of forcefulness and revenge, maintaining selfless love and pity for all living things. Man is born good, and evil appears only when harmony falls apart. A person evolves spiritually if he lives right and selflessly.

Endless Knot, a symbol of Karma, by Wikimedia user Rickjpelle

I should emphasize that in no way am I saying that the European tradition evolved from Hindu tradition. Only that the Indo-Europeans brought their Proto-Indo-European belief system to both the West and the East. From there, each culture developed independently as their own unique culture. The two systems stem from the same parent culture.

But, when the European belief system has been fragmented and survives in smaller pieces, or encoded in the folklore in ways that may not seem blatantly obvious, sometimes it can help to look at other cultures which bear some of the legacy of the ancient cultural group which influenced both, and let it inform us to fill in a more whole understanding of the bits that are missing from our own tradition.

And, indeed, as I study the folk tradition, I find more and more that the pieces may not even be missing at all. It is only that one requires the lens through which to view them. Looking toward the cosmology of a distant cultural cousin which kept their ancient mythical inheritance more intact can help open up understanding of the framework that our own beliefs functioned within.

The Germanic tradition viewed fate as something that could be directly changed based on your personal life decisions. The Germanic people also placed a very high value on living with honor and honorable deeds. In the Baltic tradition, we see an emphasis on harmony and actively working to live within harmony of all living things. And, indeed, Trinkūnas explains that "the Golden Rule," while it is certainly found in the Christian Bible, is also found in indigenous European belief.

The Golden Rule as Karma in "The Star Money"

"The Star-Money" is a very brief narrative that functions as a didactic tale, which is a tale with a main purpose of teaching a moral lesson. This tale can be viewed within a Christian context, and indeed, the lesson of the Golden Rule is also a Biblical concept. It is often hard to say when some fairy tales originated because tales that pre-date Christian conversion will be altered by Christian storytellers, and tales that originated after conversion will be influenced by the framework in place by the tales that came before.

It is absolutely valid to read this tale as a Christian lesson in morality. But, the reason I chose to delve into the concept of Karma is because, as we have seen, the European tradition most certainly possessed analogous concepts within its own indigenous parameters of belief. In addition, Christianity often encourages being good because it is the right thing to do, and that rewards will be bestowed in Heaven; whereas this tale depicts the Golden Rule in a way that teaches that being good in mortal life will yield tangible rewards in this lifetime.

Reading this tale on its own and without background knowledge, I would absolutely say that a Christian interpretation is valid. However, if you remember from "The Three Heads of the Well," the Teutonic concept of Wyrd was encoded in the tale by the presence of the figures of the three heads, their use of the word "weird" (which was explained to be a later evolution of the word "wyrd"), their presence inside of a well, that there were three in number, and that they granted

Illustration by Heinrich Vogeler

blessings or curses that affected a person's fate, were all clues that these figures were vestigial memories of the Germanic mythical figures known as the Norns (analogous to the Greek Fates).

So, that this story is the same "type" of tale, albeit a much simplified version, where a young girl goes out into the world, has the choice of whether or not to be generous even though she does not have many possessions, and is duly rewarded for it, fits within the framework of the tales that have overt pre-Christian origins. It is likely that over time this version was whittled down to the basics, or simply inspired by other similar tales but told by a storyteller who felt it was important to frame the tale within a Christian context.

But, because this tale is clearly a tale about "do unto others," and because we had discussed the concept of fate in terms of Germanic Wyrd in Volume I of this series, it is relevant that the concept of one's actions affecting their fate and destiny was widespread in the European tradition; and, indeed, seems to have clear origins in our own ancient Proto-Indo-European mythical inheritance.

We do not necessarily need to look to the East for spiritual fulfillment because of an idea that our own is somehow lacking. However, when we understand that the Indo-Europeans were the mother culture which birthed the majority of European languages and had a major influence on most European mythologies, and when we know that we have culturally experienced a separation from our indigenous spirituality, by looking at a living tradition that never died out and is descended from the same ancient parent as ours, it can help give us new eyes to see the rich treasures found within our own tradition.

As we continue through this series, we will be attempting to tease out more and more indigenous European worldview, cultural values, and spiritual beliefs that seem to have lived on very strongly in our folk tradition. But, being as informed as possible about our own mythologies, and the mythologies of related cultures (even when that link is very far removed), sometimes helps us see something right under our noses that we might have overlooked.

The Three Fates by Paul Thumann

The Star Money

Once upon a time there was a little girl whose mother and father had died and she was all alone. She had no brothers or sisters, no aunts or uncles, or grandparents to care for her. She soon became so poor that she could not pay for a room to live in and had no bed to sleep in at night. Soon, her money ran out and she had to sell all of the things that she and her parents had owned, so she was left with nothing except the clothes she was wearing.

Art by William-Adolphe Bouguereau

The little girl was very good and always tried to do the right thing. And as she stood alone in the street, a kind stranger took pity on her and gave her a piece of bread. With only this in her hand, she decided to leave the village and walk down the road into the countryside, trusting that the good God would help her on her path.

Soon she came across an old man who was a beggar, and he said to her, "please, will you give me something to eat? I am so hungry!"

Art by Ivan Kramskoy

And so, the little girl reached into to her pocket and took out the last of her bread and, with sincere kindness in her heart, she handed it over to the old man and said, "May the good God bless it to your use." She smiled at him, and then walked on.

She walked on and on, and soon she came across someone else. This time it was a little orphan boy who looked very cold. When she approached him, he said, "My head is so cold! Please will you give me something to cover it with?"

The Beggar Boy by John Opie

The little girl immediately removed the only hood that she had, which was keeping her own had warm, and she handed it to the boy. With joy in her heart she said, "May the good God bless it to your use." And then she walked on

On and on she walked, and soon she met another child who had no jacket. By now, it was starting to get dark and it was very cold. But, the little girl took off her jacket and gave it happily to the child, for he seemed much more cold than she.

Further down the road she walked, until she was met yet again by another little girl who had no frock to wear over her petticoats. And so, without a second thought, the good little girl took off her own dress and gave it to the stranger child with her blessing.

The little girl kept walking until the path led into a forest. By now, it was very dark outside. So, when yet another poor child came along and begged for a shirt, the little girl thought, "Well, it is so dark that no one will see me, I can give away my own shirt." And so, she took that off also and gave it away, too.

And now the little girl stood all alone in the very dark woods and she had not one single thing left except for her petticoat that she had worn under her clothes. She had no food, no warm clothes, no money, and no bed to sleep in for the night.

Suddenly, she heard the most beautiful sound, like tinkling chimes, and little fairy lights started falling from the sky down through the forest trees. The stars themselves were raining stardust down all around her. But, as the glowing shards of light landed upon the ground, each one turned into a shining gold coin!

Vintage postcard by O. Herrfurth

The little girl could not believe her eyes. For, one moment she was very cold in only her undergarments, and the next moment she was dressed in a beautiful new dress of shining silk! A warm jacket then appeared, and a pair of cozy boots to warm her toes. She squealed with happiness and picked up the gold coins, gathering them into her brand new apron.

For every day afterward, the little girl was never cold or hungry again. For as long as she continued to be good to others, the stars above continued to bless her with all that she could ever need.

THE END

Illustration by Viktor Paul Mohn

Bibliography and Further Reading:

Anthony, David W. *The horse, the wheel, and language : how bronze-age riders from the Eurasian steppes shaped the modern world.* Princeton: Princeton University Press, 2010.

Bates, Brian. *The Real Middle Earth.* Oxford: Sidgwick& Jackson, 2002.

Hayden, Brian. *Shamans, Sorcerers, and Saints: A Prehistory of Religion.* . Smithsonian Institution, 2003.

Simpson, Jacqueline. *European Mythology.* London: The Hamlyn Publishing Group, 1987.

Trinkūnas, Jonas. *Baltic Religion Today.* Vilnius: Romuva, 2011.

Various. *Grimm's Fairy Tales.* Ed. Frances Jenkins Olcott. Philadelphia: The Penn Publishing Company, 1927.

About the Author:

Carolyn Emerick writes about the history, mythology, and folk belief of Northwestern Europe. She has a bachelor's degree in English literature, and possesses a lifelong learning and love of European cultural heritage.

Learn more at:

www.CarolynEmerick.com

Sign up for more books like this for $1 at:

www.Patreon.com/CarolynEmerick

Follow on Facebook at:

www.Facebook.com/CarolynEmerick.writer

Made in the USA
Monee, IL
27 December 2022

23556192R00029